THE
MAGNIFICENT
❧ BOOK ❧
OF
EXTINCT ANIMALS

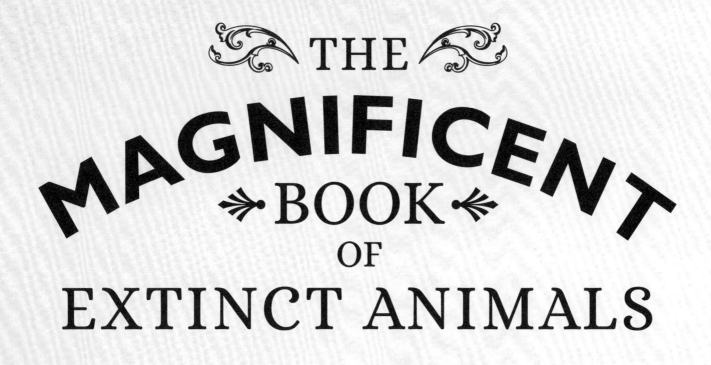

THE MAGNIFICENT
BOOK
OF
EXTINCT ANIMALS

ILLUSTRATED BY
Val Walerczuk

WRITTEN BY
Barbara Taylor

Written by Barbara Taylor
Illustrated by Val Walerczuk and Pino Avonto

Published by Weldon Owen Children's Books
An imprint of Weldon Owen International, L.P.
A subsidiary of Insight International, L.P.
PO Box 3088
San Rafael, CA 94912
www.insighteditions.com

Weldon Owen Children's Books:
Designed by Bryn Walls
Edited by Diana Craig
Art director: Stuart Smith
Senior Prodcution Manager: Greg Steffen
Publisher: Sue Grabham

Insight Editions:
Publisher: Raoul Goff

ISBN: 978-1-68188-737-1
Manufactured, printed, and assembled in China.
First printing, November 2021
26 25 24 3 4 5 6 7 8

Introduction

Our planet is home to creatures of every kind. For hundreds of millions of years, animals have filled each corner of the world—from rainforest to desert, grassland to rocky coast, thermal springs to wide rivers. Over time many species have become extinct, while new ones have appeared. But for thousands of years, people have caused animals to die out much more quickly than they naturally would.

When we turn wild areas into farmland, animals lose their homes. When we introduce animals into areas that they don't naturally live in, they prey on existing species or take their food. We have burned fuels like coal, oil, and gas, which have trapped heat in the Earth's atmosphere. This has changed the climate of our planet and caused dangerously extreme weather such as drought, fire, and flood.

The Magnificent Book of Extinct Animals brings back to life some of the wonderful animals that have been lost through human activity. From the paradise parrot to the Jamaican sunset moth, and from the Javan tiger to the Caribbean monk seal, people's actions have led to the disappearance of these magnificent creatures. It is important to understand what we have lost and why so that we can work together to preserve today's endangered animals and those of the future.

Fact file

Lived: Eastern USA

Habitat: Forests and swamps

Length: 12 in. (30 cm)

Diet: Seeds, fruits, flowers, buds

Extinct: 1918

Contents

Atlas bear

Ursus arctos crowtheri

 The Atlas bear once lived in the mighty Atlas Mountains of North Africa. In prehistoric times, this animal was believed to live all across North Africa.

 Predators such as the Barbary lion and Barbary leopard lived in the same area as the Atlas bear. The bear may have climbed up into the trees to escape attack.

 During the winter, the females gave birth to two or three tiny, blind, hairless cubs. The cubs fed on their mother's milk until spring or early summer. They stayed with their mother for several years.

 Atlas bear cubs needed to know how to hunt and defend themselves. Their mother taught them these skills, but it took up to four years for the cubs to learn.

 Atlas bears communicated with growls and grunts. They also left smelly footprints, droppings, and scratches on tree bark. Other bears understood these "messages."

Thousands of years ago, the climate in northern Africa became drier. The bears' forest home began to turn to desert and fewer Atlas bears were able to survive.

Atlas bears were gradually hunted to extinction from the time of the ancient Romans more than 2,000 years ago. The Romans hunted them for sport, and captured them to fight gladiators, lions, and tigers in Roman arenas.

Fact file

Lived: Northern Africa

Habitat: Mountains and forests

Length: 9 ft. (2.7 m)

Diet: Roots, fruits, nuts, small mammals, carrion (dead animals)

Extinct: 1890

Paradise parrot

Psephotellus pulcherrimus

- The male paradise parrot was as dazzling as a rainbow. Shimmering green and turquoise plumage covered his breast, flashes of red glowed on his head, wings and underparts, and a patch of yellow highlighted each eye.

- The females and young parrots were much less colorful than the males, which helped to camouflage them from predators.

- The second part of this bird's name, *pulcherrimus*, comes from a Latin word meaning "most beautiful."

- The paradise parrot could fly quickly, but spent almost all of its time on the ground. It fed mainly on the seeds of grasses, stripping them off the grasses with its sharp beak.

- To avoid attracting predators, the paradise parrot was very quiet while feeding on the ground. If it sensed danger, the bird would make a whistling alarm call.

Fact file

Lived: Eastern Australia

Habitat: Grassy woodlands

Length: 10½ in. (27 cm)

Diet: Grass seeds

Extinct: 1927

These incredible birds dug their nests in abandoned termite mounds. They used their sharp bills to break up the hard crust of the mound and drilled a narrow, round tunnel inside, with a larger nest chamber at the end.

People drove these parrots to extinction by catching them as pets and collecting their eggs. They used the grassland where the birds lived to rear cattle.

Javan tiger

Panthera tigris sondaica

🐆 The Javan tiger once roamed the forests of Java, an island northwest of Australia. Today, the island is one of the most crowded places on Earth. As the human population there grew, there was less and less room for this magnificent big cat.

🐆 Once, Javan tigers were found all over the island of Java. But people cleared the wild forests where the tigers lived to make space to grow rice, coffee, teak, and rubber. By the year 2003, there were no Javan tigers left.

🐆 Javan tigers were smaller than their cousins on mainland Asia. But they were very strong, and could break the legs of horses or water buffaloes with their big paws.

These big cats had slender bodies covered with a beautiful pattern of thin stripes. They also had long, skinny noses and particularly long whiskers.

Javan tigers lived on their own in a large home area, or territory. To warn other tigers away, they marked the edges of their territory by peeing on plants and scratching tree trunks.

The main prey of the Javan tiger was the Rusa deer. In the 1960s, many of these deer died because of disease, so it was difficult for the tigers to find enough to eat.

Fact file

Lived: Java, Indonesia

Habitat: Forests and mountains

Length: 6–8 ft. (2–2.5 m)

Diet: Rusa deer, wild boar, banteng (cattle), water birds, reptiles

Extinct: 2003

Xerces blue butterfly

Glaucopsyche xerces

- The male Xerces blue butterfly had shimmering, lilac-blue wings. His jewel-like coloring was designed to impress the females and to win a mate. The female needed to stay camouflaged while she laid her eggs, so her wings were brown.

- This beautiful butterfly was named after King Xerxes of Persia (modern-day Iran). King Xerxes ruled his kingdom nearly 2,500 years ago.

- Female Xerces blues laid their eggs on deerweed and lupin plants. The caterpillars had an instant food supply as soon as they hatched.

- Ants that lived alongside the caterpillar helped to keep predators away. In return, the caterpillar produced a sugary food on its back for the ants to eat.

Fact file

Lived: San Francisco Bay Area, California, USA

Habitat: Coastal sand dunes

Wingspan: 1–1¼ in (2.8–3 cm)

Diet: Lupins, deerweed (caterpillars); flower nectar (adults)

Extinct: 1941–1943

The last Xerces blues died out less than 80 years ago. People had collected the butterflies and destroyed the places where they lived. Farm animals also ate the plants where the females laid their eggs.

Pyrenean ibex

Capra pyrenaica pyrenaica

 This agile wild goat could easily clamber up the steep cliffs of its rugged mountain home. Its hooves had sharp edges and hollow undersides. They worked a bit like suction cups, helping the ibex to grip onto sheer rockfaces.

 The spectacular curved horns of the male ibex had thick ridges along the front. Each ridge represented roughly a year's growth so gave a clue to the male's age.

 Male Pyrenean ibex had to fight for the right to mate with the females. They head-butted each other with their massive curved horns. Their skulls were extra-strong to take all the battering.

Female Pyrenean ibex gave birth to one baby called a kid in May or early June. The little kids could walk within just a day of being born.

Fact file

Location: Pyrenees in Spain, France, Andorra

Habitat: Rocky mountains with cliffs, trees and meadows

Length: 5 ft. (1.5 m)

Diet: Leaves, grasses, bushes

Extinct: 2000

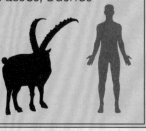

Winter in the Pyrenees can be freezing cold, so the ibex grew a long, thick winter coat to keep warm. In summer, its coat was shorter and thinner, and it climbed higher up the mountains.

Pyrenean ibex had to be on the alert for predators such as golden eagles or wolves. They had excellent eyesight and keen senses of smell and hearing.

Around 120 years ago, there were fewer than 100 ibex left. By 2000 they had died out completely. Hunters killed them for their horns, people turned their mountain home into farmland, and sheep and cattle competed with the ibex for food.

Lesser bilby

Macrotis leucura

- The lesser bilby was about as big as a small rabbit, with a tail more than half as long as its body. Its pointed, rabbitlike ears were always twitching to pick up the smallest sound.

- This little animal was an expert at digging tunnels. It used its strong front legs and stout, curved claws to burrow into sand dunes. It could dig tunnels up to 10 ft. (3 m) long and 5 ft. (1.5 m) deep.

- These shy animals came out at night. They spent the day inside their burrows, sealing the entrance with loose sand to keep predators out.

- Lesser bilbies slept sitting up, with their pointed nose tucked between their legs and their long ears folded over their eyes.

- The lesser bilby was a marsupial, or animal with a pouch on its belly. Baby bilbies stayed tucked safely inside their mother's pouch for the first ten weeks of life.

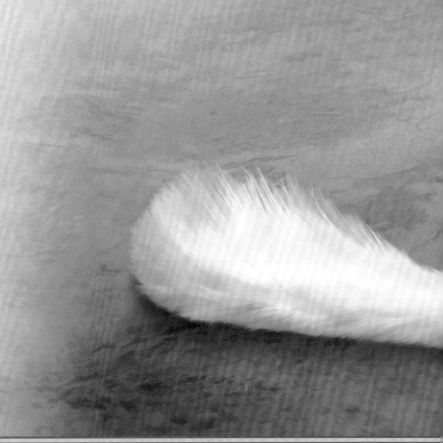

Fact file

Lived: Central Australia

Habitat: Desert, grassland, woodland

Length: 7¾–10½ in. (20–27 cm)

Diet: Ants, termites, roots, seeds, fruit, small mammals

Extinct: 1950s–1960s

Lesser bilbies did not need to drink water. They got all the water they needed from their food.

Lesser bilbies became extinct when they were killed by other animals that people introduced, such as red foxes and cats. People also hunted lesser bilbies for their smooth, silky fur.

Quagga

Equus quagga quagga

🦓 The quagga was a type of zebra. Around 150 years ago, it roamed the southern African plains, munching on grass and leaves. Its call sounded like "Kwa-ka-ka," which gave the animal its name.

🦓 Quaggas lived alongside ostriches and wildebeest. Together, they helped keep each other safe by using different senses to detect danger. The ostrich used its eyesight, the wildebeest its sense of smell, and the quagga its excellent hearing.

🦓 These zebras fed during the day and rested at night. After darkness fell, at least one member of the herd stayed on guard to watch for predators, such as lions.

🦓 If a quagga was sick or injured, the rest of the herd looked after it.

🦓 Quaggas nibbled each other's necks, manes, and backs to remove harmful parasites. Sometimes the quaggas let oxpecker birds ride on their backs. The birds ate the parasites and cleaned the quaggas' coats for them.

Fact file

Lived: Southern Africa

Habitat: Grasslands, scrubland

Length: 8½ ft. (2.6 m)

Diet: Grass, leaves, fruit

Extinct: 1878

Quagga foals could run within an hour of being born. This helped them to keep up with the herd when it was on the move, and avoid danger. The foals drank their mother's milk for nearly a year but could eat grass at one week old.

People drove quaggas to extinction through hunting. They killed them for food, and for their skin, which was made into bags to carry grain. Farmers killed quaggas because they ate the grass needed for sheep and goats.

Steller's sea cow

Hydrodamalis gigas

Fact file

Lived: Northern Pacific Ocean

Habitat: Shallow coastal waters

Length: 30 ft. (9 m)

Diet: Seaweed (mostly kelp) and seagrass

Extinct: 1768

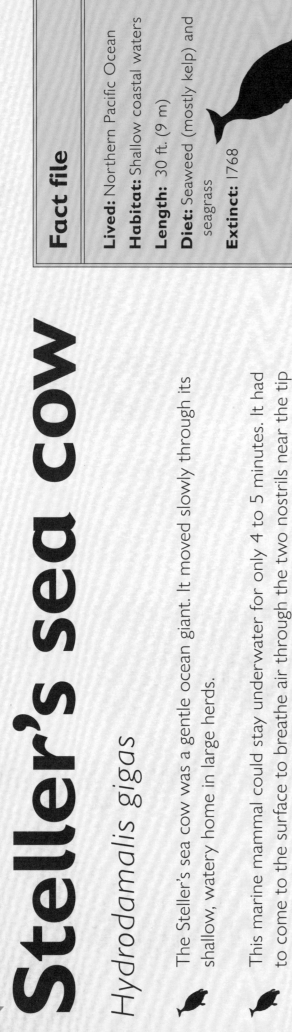

🐟 The Steller's sea cow was a gentle ocean giant. It moved slowly through its shallow, watery home in large herds.

🐟 This marine mammal could stay underwater for only 4 to 5 minutes. It had to come to the surface to breathe air through the two nostrils near the tip of its snout.

🐟 The Steller's sea cow had a wide, flat tail that it flapped up and down to push itself through the water, as whales do today.

🐟 This sea cow used its stumpy, hooklike flippers to help it make its way across rocks, or to hold onto the rocks when the sea was rough.

🐟 A "padded coat" kept this sea cow warm in the cold waters where it lived. A thick layer of fatty blubber just under its skin stopped the heat escaping from its body.

🐟 Instead of teeth, this sea cow had horny pads in its mouth, with ridges for mashing up seaweed. The large gut inside its big belly helped the animal to digest its tough food.

🐟 This sea cow's thick, wrinkled outer skin helped to prevent it from injuring

People hunted Steller's sea cows to extinction. They ate their meat and used their leathery skin to cover boats and make shoes and belts. People also turned the sea cows' fat into oil to burn in lamps.

Great auk

Pinguinus impennis

The great auk had tiny wings and could not fly. With its white chest and black "jacket," it looked like a giant penguin. But great auks were not related to penguins, although they had a similar lifestyle.

On land, great auks walked upright, waddling along slowly and flapping their stubby wings to help them clamber up steep slopes. They walked at about the same speed as a person, so were easy for hunters to catch.

In the ocean, the great auk was a fast and graceful swimmer, diving to catch fish underwater. It could hold its breath for up to 15 minutes. Webbed feet helped it to swim faster, like a person using flippers.

A layer of fat under their thick feathers helped to keep great auks warm in cold oceans and during freezing weather on land.

The heavy, curved bill of the great auk was nearly as long as a child's hand. It had eight or more grooves on the end.

Huge colonies of great auks nested together on steep, rocky islands near the ocean. Here, they were safe from polar bears and other land predators.

Pairs of male and female great auks stayed together for life. The female laid only one egg at a time. Both parents kept the egg warm and looked after the egg until it hatched.

The last great auks died out nearly 200 years ago. The birds were driven to extinction by people hunting them for food or for their eggs, feathers, and fat. Many birds and their eggs were also collected for museums.

Fact file

Lived: North Atlantic Ocean

Habitat: Oceans and rocky coasts

Height: 30–33 in. (75–85 cm)

Diet: Fish and plankton

Extinct: 1844

Golden toad

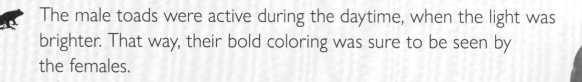

Incilius periglenes

 The shiny, bright-orange skin of the male golden toad was meant to get him noticed and make him stand out against the green of the forest. It was his way of showing himself off to the females and attracting a mate.

 The male toads were active during the daytime, when the light was brighter. That way, their bold coloring was sure to be seen by the females.

Male golden toads were quieter than many other male frogs and toads. They did not have a vocal sac, or throat pouch, that they could blow up to make their calls boom out into the forest.

The female golden toad was greenish-yellow and black with red spots. She blended in with her forest background.

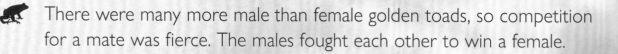

There were many more male than female golden toads, so competition for a mate was fierce. The males fought each other to win a female.

Fact file

Lived: Costa Rica

Habitat: Rainforest

Length: Female 1½–2 in. (42–56 mm); male 1½–1¾ in. (39–48 mm)

Diet: Small insects and other invertebrates

Extinct: 2004

Golden toads hid underground in moist burrows for most of the year. In the wet season, from March to June, they left their burrows to find a mate and to lay their eggs.

These tiny toads mated and laid their eggs in pools of rainwater that formed among tree roots in the wet season. The females laid 200 to 400 eggs at a time.

In 1987, there were about 1,500 living adult toads, but just a few years later, there were no toads left. Scientists are not sure why this happened. Climate change, air pollution, and disease could have been among the causes.

Toolache wallaby

Notamacropus greyi

 The toolache, or Grey's, wallaby, was a champion athlete. It could bound along at high speed on its powerful back legs, and jump long distances. This helped it to escape predators.

The long tail of the toolache wallaby worked like an extra limb. It helped the wallaby to balance when it moved about, and gave the animal extra support when it sat upright.

Female toolache wallabies, or fliers, protected their tiny newborns inside a warm pouch on the front of their bodies. Safe inside, the babies, or joeys, drank milk from their mothers.

The toolache wallaby had to watch out for eagles, wild dogs, and other predators. It used its clawed feet and strong legs to give these attackers a mighty kick. Males also kicked each other during battles over females.

Toolache wallabies died out just over 80 years ago. They were hunted for their beautiful fur, and much of the open grassland where they lived was turned into farmland.

Fact file

Lived: Southern Australia

Habitat: Open grassland

Length: 32–33 in. (81–84 cm)

Diet: Grass, leaves, roots

Extinct: 1939

Tecopa pupfish

Cyprinodon nevadensis calidae

- This tough little fish lived in Tecopa Hot Springs in California's Mojave Desert. The temperature of the water there could reach 110° F (43° C), which is as warm as a hot bath. This would have killed most other fish.

- In colder winter weather, the pupfish burrowed into the mud to keep warm. In the hot summer, it often moved into deeper, cooler water to escape from the sun and heat.

- The pupfish got its name because of the way it sometimes waved its tail, rather like the wagging tail of a puppy.

- In the breeding season, the male turned a brilliant blue to attract the attention of the females and to find a mate.

- Female Tecopa pupfish were striped and olive-brown. These colors and markings gave the females good camouflage.

Tecopa pupfish probably lived for no more than two years and reproduced slowly. Only two to ten babies hatched from their eggs every year.

This pupfish became extinct after people turned Tecopa Hot Springs into a holiday resort. They also introduced other fish, bullfrogs, and crayfish, which ate the pupfish and competed with them for food.

Fact file

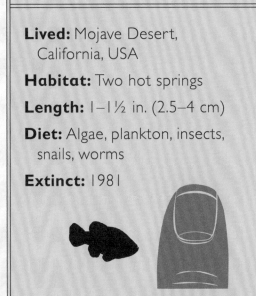

Lived: Mojave Desert, California, USA

Habitat: Two hot springs

Length: 1–1½ in. (2.5–4 cm)

Diet: Algae, plankton, insects, snails, worms

Extinct: 1981

Lyall's wren

Traversia lyalli

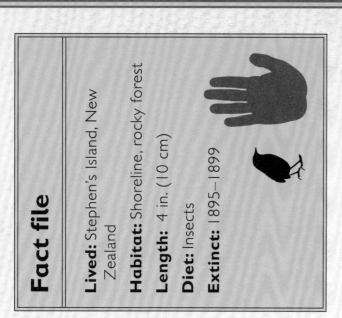

Fact file

Lived: Stephen's Island, New Zealand

Habitat: Shoreline, rocky forest

Length: 4 in. (10 cm)

Diet: Insects

Extinct: 1895–1899

Lyall's wren was the smallest flightless bird to have ever existed. It weighed only around ¾ oz (23 g), which is about as heavy as two tablespoons of sugar.

This tiny songbird was more like a mouse than a bird. It scurried quickly along the ground on its big feet, looking for food inside logs or among piles of rocks.

The wings of a Lyall's wren were too small and weak for flying, but it may have feebly flapped its wings to help it to jump.

Male Lyall's wrens had yellow-green feathers, while the females were a brownish-grey.

Lyall's wrens did not need to fly to find food. There was plenty to eat on the ground all year round. The little birds had no predators to escape from, until cats arrived.

These wrens were hunted to extinction by the cats that people brought to their island. About five years after the cats arrived, there were no Lyall's wrens left.

Lyall's wrens are named after David Lyall, a lighthouse keeper on Stephen's Island who studied these little birds.

O'ahu tree snail

Achatinella apexfulva

- More than 40 kinds of tree snail like this once lived on the Hawaiian island of O'ahu, but many have already died out. The people of Hawaii believed that the snails sang as they moved about and called them "the voice of the forest."

- During the day, the O'ahu tree snail sealed itself tightly inside its shell. At night, it came out to graze on fungi and algae on the forest leaves.

- The O'ahu tree snail did not reproduce until it was at least five years old, and then it gave birth to only one baby snail at a time. The tiny babies were about the size of a child's little fingernail.

- People collected O'ahu tree snails for their beautiful striped shells. They also cut down the forests when the snails lived.

Fact file

Lived: O'ahu, Hawaii

Habitat: Tropical forest

Length: ¾ in. (2 cm)

Diet: Fungi, algae

Extinct: 2019

In 1955, the rosy wolf snail was introduced to Hawaii to prey on the giant African snails that were eating the crops. But this fierce predator ate many O'ahu tree snails, too. It was the main cause of the snails' extinction.

The last of this species of tree snail was born in captivity at the University of Hawaii after his parents were collected from the wild. He was called George. He lived for 14 years but died on New Year's Day in 2019.

Pinta Island tortoise

Chelonoidis abingdonii

- Pinta Island tortoises could weigh as much as three people. These giants lived for up to 200 years and continued to grow throughout their lives.

- Each day, the Pinta Island tortoise spent about 16 hours resting and sunbathing. For the remaining time, it munched away at plants with its sharp, toothless beak.

- This tortoise had a shell that curved upward at the front, like a horse's saddle. This allowed its long neck to move freely and stretch up to reach taller plants, such as juicy cactus pads.

Fact file

Lived: Pinta Island in the Galapagos Islands, Ecuador

Habitat: Scrubland

Length: 4–5 ft. (1.2–1.5 m)

Diet: Grass, fruits, cactus

Extinct: 2012

🐢 Pinta Island tortoises could survive for a year or more without food or water. This was because their bodies worked very slowly and could store water inside.

🐢 About 2,500 giant tortoises once lived on Pinta Island, but people wiped them out. They killed the tortoises for their meat and their oil. Sailors also brought goats to the island, which ate the tortoises' food.

🐢 The last Pinta Island giant tortoise was about 100 years old when he died in 2012. This famous tortoise was nicknamed Lonesome George because he was the last of his kind.

Chinese paddlefish

Psephurus gladius

- This ancient river creature was alive at the time of the dinosaurs. It survived for more than 200 million years, but died out in this century.

- The Chinese paddlefish once swam in the mighty Yangtze River in China. It could not see well in the muddy river waters. Instead, the paddlefish used its swordlike snout to detect electrical signals given off by prey.

- A strong swimmer and top predator, the paddlefish used its powerful jaws to catch its prey, such as fish.

Fact file

Lived: China

Habitat: River, lakes, coasts

Length: 10 ft. (3 m)

Diet: Fish, crabs, shrimp

Extinct: 2005–2010

The Chinese paddlefish was one of the largest freshwater fish in the world. It was as long as a small car.

The female paddlefish laid thousands of eggs at a time. The eggs hatched into tiny fish after a few days. The baby fish, called fries, gathered together in schools for protection. This made them easy for fishermen to catch.

Chinese paddlefish were a favorite dish of ancient Chinese emperors. The paddlefish's eggs were also made into an expensive snack called caviar for people to eat.

People drove the Chinese paddlefish to extinction by catching so many of them to eat. People also built big dams on the Yangtze River, which stopped the paddlefish reaching the places where they laid their eggs.

Christmas Island pipistrelle

Pipistrellus murrayi

- This little bat would have fit in the palm of your hand. It was the smallest known bat in Australia.

- The Christmas Island pipistrelle lived on one small island in the Indian Ocean. The island was given its name by an English sea captain who sailed by on Christmas Day in 1643.

- Christmas Island pipistrelles roosted, or rested, in tree hollows or under the bark of dead trees. They also sheltered under strangler figs or dead palm leaves.

- At night, this tiny bat zoomed through the air at high speed to catch flying insects such as moths, beetles, and flying ants.

- Like many other bats, these pipistrelles used echoes to locate prey and find their way around in the dark. They made high-pitched sounds that bounced back off things around them and told the bats where these objects were.

- Female Christmas Island pipistrelles gave birth to just one baby each year. The baby bats drank their mother's milk for about four weeks.

- Christmas Island pipistrelles began to die out when their rainforest home was cleared for mining. They were also killed by wolf snakes, giant centipedes, rats, cats, and other predators that arrived on the island with human settlers.

Fact file

Lived: Christmas Island, Australia

Habitat: Rainforest

Length: 1–1½ in. (35–40 mm)

Diet: Flying insects

Extinct: 2009

O‘ahu honeycreeper

Akialoa ellisiana

 The O‘ahu honeycreeper crept along branches and tree trunks using its long, thin, curved bill to pry out insects. It also probed deep into tube-shaped flowers to reach the sweet nectar, or honey, inside.

 This colorful bird lived only on the Hawaiian island of O‘ahu. It is also known as the O‘ahu akialoa.

 As it carefully searched for food, the O‘ahu honeycreeper turned its head from side to side. Sometimes it even turned its head completely upside down to look underneath branches.

 O‘ahu honeycreepers sometimes drank dew or wate from wet leaves.

Fact file

Lived: O‘ahu, Hawaii

Habitat: Mountain forest

Length: 6¾–7½ in (17–19 cm)

Diet: Insects, spiders, nectar

Extinct: 2016

On rare occasions, the Oʻahu honeycreeper flew to the ground in search of prey and to pick up small stones. It swallowed the stones to help grind up food inside its gizzard, which was part of its stomach.

This honeycreeper became extinct after people cut down the forests where it lived. It also died out because of new diseases that people brought to the island, such as bird flu. The honeycreeper could not fight off these diseases.

Bubal hartebeest

Alcelaphus buselaphus buselaphus

 This elegant antelope was once found all across northern Africa, to the north of the Sahara. It also lived in the Middle East, in countries such as Israel and Jordan.

 Large herds of 100 to 200 bubal hartebeest lived together. While the herd was feeding, one hartebeest kept a lookout for danger, sometimes standing on a termite mound or rock to get a better view.

 Bubals relied on their keen eyesight to spot predators. They snorted to warn each other of danger, and then the whole herd would quickly run away in single file.

The bubal was built for speed. Its long legs allowed it to race along at the speed of a greyhound, at up to about 43 miles (70 km) per hour.

Both male and female bubals had curvy horns, which they used to fight predators. Males also clashed their formidable horns together in noisy battles to decide who would mate with the females.

Fact file

Lived: Northern Africa

Habitat: Dry, rocky grassland, forests, mountains

Length: 5–8 ft. (1.5–2.5 m)

Diet: Grasses

Extinct: 1945–1954

The female bubal hartebeest gave birth to one calf at a time in bushes away from the herd. The little calf stayed hidden there on its own for two weeks. Its mother visited every so often so that it could drink her milk.

The bubal hartebeest died out because it was hunted for its meat and horns. People also began to graze their cattle on the grasslands where the bubal lived, so there was less for the bubal to eat.

Dodo

Raphus cucullatus

 This giant flightless pigeon lived on the remote island of Mauritius. The island lies far out in the Indian Ocean, about 1,250 miles (2,000 kilometres) off the east coast of Africa.

 The dodo had stubby, useless wings and lived on the ground. It did not need to fly to find food or escape danger. There was plenty to eat on the ground and no predators on the island until people arrived.

 Dodos were once believed to be slow, tubby, and clumsy. But really, they were agile, athletic, and intelligent, with large brains. They strode about on their sturdy legs, using their keen sense of smell to sniff out food.

 The dodo's big hooked bill could give a sharp bite.

The first people to discover Mauritius set foot on the island in 1598. Dodos had never met people before, so they were not afraid of them. This made these big birds easy to catch.

Fact file

Lived: Mauritius, Indian Ocean

Habitat: Tropical forest

Length: 27½ in. (70 cm)

Diet: Fruits, nuts, seeds, roots

Extinct: 1690

People caused the dodo to die out. Sailors and settlers killed the bird for food and brought new animals to the island. These animals ate the dodo's eggs, competed with the bird for food, and destroyed the forests where it lived.

Caribbean monk seal

Neomonachus tropicalis

 These seals were acrobats in the water. They could dive down to nearly 500 feet (150 m), 70 times deeper than an Olympic swimming pool. Some monk seals plunged even further, to more than 1,800 feet (550 m).

 Sensitive whiskers on the monk seal's face helped it to sense fish and other food in the water.

Like other seals, the Caribbean monk seal was clumsy on land. It shunted itself slowly across the surface, using its front flippers to help pull its heavy body forward.

Newborn monk seal pups had a black fur coat, which helped them to keep warm. They fed on their mother's milk for about six weeks.

Fact file

Lived: Caribbean Sea, Gulf of Mexico, western Atlantic Ocean

Habitat: Oceans, coastlines, coral reefs

Length: 7–7¾ ft (2.2–2.4 m)

Diet: Fish, octopus, lobsters

Extinct: 2008

This inquisitive seal was not afraid of humans, so it was easy to catch. People turned its fatty blubber into oil for lamps and cooking. They also polluted the places where it lived. By 2008, the Caribbean monk seal had become extinct.

Rocky Mountain locust

Melanoplus spretus

Fact file

Lived: Western USA and Canada

Habitat: Mountains, grassland

Length: ¾–1¼ in. (2–3.5 cm)

Diet: Grass and other plants

Extinct: 2014

⚘ Rocky Mountain locusts traveled in gigantic swarms made up of billions of insects. The swarms could be so big that they covered the sky like storm clouds, blotting out the sun for days.

⚘ In 1875, a vast swarm of Rocky Mountain locusts was reported. Covering 200,000 square miles (over 500,000 sq. km), it was the largest locust swarm ever seen. Less than 30 years later, this locust was extinct.

⚘ These locusts were always hungry. They devoured farmers' grain and cereal crops. They also ate fence posts, sheep's wool, blankets, and washing hung out to dry. Sometimes they even ate each other.

⚘ The Rocky Mountain locusts used to "talk" to each other using sounds made by rubbing their back legs together.

⚘ Millions of Rocky Mountain locusts were blown high into the mountains and preserved in the ice of mountain glaciers. These glaciers are called "grasshopper glaciers."

Farmers probably caused the Rocky Mountain locust to die out. They plowed the land and grazed their animals in mountain valleys near where these insects laid their eggs.

Tasmanian tiger

Thylacinus cynocephalus

 The Tasmanian tiger, or thylacine, looked like a jumble of other animals stitched together. It had the body of a large dog with the head of a wolf. Tigerlike stripes covered its back and its tail, which was stiff like the tail of a kangaroo.

 Tasmanian tigers could stand on their back legs and travel short distances by hopping like a kangaroo. If they were in danger, they could bark like a dog.

Fact file

Lived: Australia, Tasmania, New Guinea

Habitat: Dry forests, grasslands, wetlands

Length: 5 ft. (1.5 m)

Diet: Small mammals such as wallabies and possums, birds

Extinct: 1982

These animals were marsupials, or mammals with pouches, like kangaroos. The female could keep two to four babies snug in her warm pouch until they were three or four months old. As the babies grew, the pouch expanded to give them more room.

Tasmanian tigers hunted mostly at night, sneaking up on their prey in a surprise attack. They could open their jaws wide but had a weak bite, which meant that these animals could only tackle smaller prey.

The Tasmanian tiger died out largely because it was hunted and its habitat was destroyed. Hotter, drier weather due to climate change also made it harder for the animal to survive.

Chinese river dolphin

Lipotes vexillifer

- For millions of years, Chinese river dolphins lived in the mighty Yangtze River in China. But in just over 50 years, people completely wiped them out.

- Chinese river dolphins usually lived in small groups of two to six individuals, but sometimes gathered in larger numbers of up to 10, or even 16 animals.

- To escape danger, these river dolphins could speed through the water at about 35 mph (60 kph), which is eight times swifter than the fastest human swimmer. Usually, they swam at 19–25 mph (30–40 kph).

- The Chinese river dolphin had tiny eyes. In the muddy, murky waters of the Yangtze River, good eyesight was not important for this dolphin.

- Using its long, sensitive snout, the Chinese river dolphin felt for its fishy prey in the muddy riverbed. It also caught fish near the surface of the water.

Fact file

Lived: China

Habitat: Rivers and lakes

Length: 7½–8¼ ft (2.3–2.5 m)

Diet: Fish

Extinct: 2004

Chinese river dolphins used clicking sounds to find their way around. The echoes that bounced back helped the animals to find fish and avoid predators. But the echoes were harder to hear once the river became full of noisy ships.

These dolphins couldn't survive in the busy, polluted waters of the Yangtze River. Millions of people had come to live near the river. They built dams across the water and factories along the banks. They used boats and explosives to catch fish.

Alaotra grebe

Tachybaptus rufolavatus

- The wide, shallow, marshy waters of Lake Alaotra were once home to this small grebe. This lake is on the island of Madagascar, which is off the southeast coast of Africa.

- The Alaotra grebe was sometimes known as the rusty grebe because of its reddish feathers. It was also called Delacour's little grebe. Jean Delacour was the scientist who first identified the bird in 1932.

- Short wings meant that this little waterbird could not fly far away. It stayed close to home on Lake Alaotra.

- The irises, or colored parts, of the Alaotra grebe's eyes were pale yellow, making them stand out like two bright buttons.

- To catch fish, the Alaotra grebe dived down among the reeds and other water plants on the lakeshore. It often fished with other species of grebes.

Fact file

Lived: Madagascar
Habitat: Lakes and marshes
Length: 10 in. (25 cm)
Diet: Fish
Extinct: 2010

Alaotra grebes usually lived in male-and-female pairs. In the breeding season, the birds had a dark, blackish cap on their head and rusty-brown feathers on their throat and around their ears.

The Alaotra grebe could not survive all the threats it faced. Marshy areas around the lake were converted to rice farms. The bird was hunted for food and drowned in fishing nets. The young were caught by new fish that people introduced to the lake.

Jamaican sunset moth

Urania sloanus

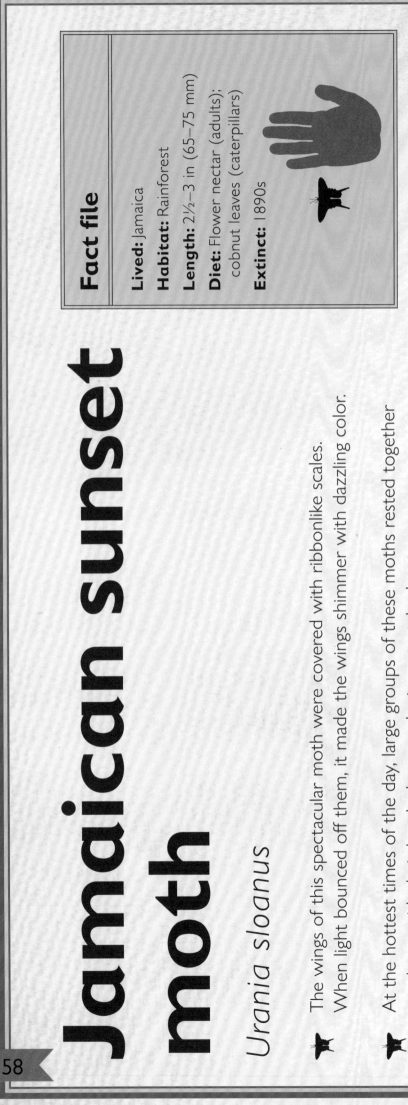

Fact file

Lived: Jamaica

Habitat: Rainforest

Length: 2½–3 in (65–75 mm)

Diet: Flower nectar (adults);
cobnut leaves (caterpillars)

Extinct: 1890s

➤ The wings of this spectacular moth were covered with ribbonlike scales. When light bounced off them, it made the wings shimmer with dazzling color.

➤ At the hottest times of the day, large groups of these moths rested together on plants, with their heads down and wings stretched out.

➤ Jamaican sunset moth caterpillars fed on poisonous leaves. This did not harm the caterpillars, but it made them toxic to predators.

➤ Like the caterpillars, adult Jamaican sunset moths were poisonous. Their bright colors warned predators that they were dangerous to eat.

➤ This moth became extinct when the forests where it lived were cut down. The land was used to grow crops instead. The caterpillars could no longer find enough of their special food plants to eat.

Bramble Cay melomys

Melomys rubicola

- This little mammal lived on a very small, flat coral island, or cay, called Bramble Cay. The island lies at the northern tip of the Great Barrier Reef off the eastern coast of Australia.

- The Bramble Cay melomys was only half as heavy as a hamster.

- Scales arranged in a mosaic pattern covered the melomys' tail. This gave the animal its other name, the Bramble Cay mosaic-tailed rat.

- The Bramble Cay melomys dug burrows under plants or lived under leaves or branches on the ground. It came out at night to eat fleshy herbs or green turtle eggs.

The island where the melomys once lived is only just above sea level. At its highest point, it is 10 feet (3 metres) tall, which is not much higher than an average door. Wind and waves change the island's shape all the time.

The melomys was the first mammal to become extinct because of climate change. Rising sea levels and tropical storms have flooded the cay many times, destroying the animal's habitat and drowning the animals themselves.

Fact file

Lived: Australia

Habitat: Grassland

Length: 6–6½ in. (15–16.5 cm)

Diet: Plants, eggs

Extinct: 2015–2019

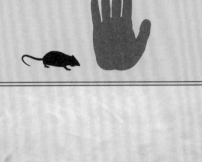

Yunnan lake newt

Cynops wolterstorffi

The Yunnan lake newt had a bright red or orange belly with black markings, which is why it was known as a firebelly newt. The red and black markings warned predators that its skin was poisonous.

This large newt was found along the shores of a lake near Kunming, in Yunnan, southern China. It lived among the plants in the shallows, as well as in irrigation canals, ponds, and swamps.

In the breeding season, thousands of Yunnan lake newts gathered together to mate. The males showed off to the females by fanning their deep-blue tails, which changed colour for the breeding season.

In the cold winter months, Yunnan lake newts moved into the deeper waters of the lake and went into a deep sleep, or hibernation.

As cities grew around Kunming Lake, its waters were polluted by industrial and farming waste, and sewage. Many of the newts died because they absorbed the poisonous water through their smooth skin.

Yunnan lake newts were crowded out of their home after people introduced ducks, exotic fish, and bullfrogs to the lake. The newts could not compete with these new arrivals for food and living spaces.

Fact file

Lived: China

Habitat: Lake shores, canals, ponds, swamps

Length: 4¾–6 in (12–16 cm)

Diet: Tadpoles, shrimp, water creatures, worms, insects

Extinct: 1979

South Island giant moa

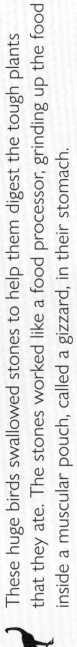

Dinornis robustus

- This giant, flightless bird had shaggy feathers and was twice as tall as an ostrich. There were at least nine other types of moa living in New Zealand at the same time. This moa was the biggest of them all.

- The South Island giant moa had no wing bones at all. But it did have three extra neck bones to support its very long neck.

- Female giant moas could be more than twice the size of males and weighed as much as a cow.

- This moa could run very fast on its long legs to escape from predators, such as Haast's eagles. If it couldn't escape, this powerful bird could kick its attacker with its strong feet.

- These huge birds swallowed stones to help them digest the tough plants that they ate. The stones worked like a food processor, grinding up the food inside a muscular pouch, called a gizzard, in their stomach.

- South Island giant moas became extinct within a few hundred years of people arriving in New Zealand from Polynesia. The name *moa* comes from a Polynesian word for "fowl."

These moas died out mainly
because people hunted
them and collected
their eggs. People also
destroyed their habitat.

Fact file

Lived: South Island, New Zealand

Habitat: Shrubland, duneland,
grassland, forest

Height: 12 ft. (3.6 m)

Diet: Twigs, leaves, flowers, berries,
seeds

Extinct: 1400–1445

St. Helena giant earwig

Labidura herculeana

- This supersized insect was the world's largest earwig. It was about as large as the palm of an adult's hand.

- The earwig was found on a small, remote island called St. Helena in the South Atlantic Ocean. It lived in a deep burrow underneath the rocky ground.

- The St. Helena giant earwig came out at night or after the summer rains. If it was threatened, it quickly ran back into its burrow. The earwig's flat body helped it to fit into tight spaces.

- To scare off predators, the earwig raised up the fearsome pincers on the back of its body. It also used its pincers to catch prey. Males fought each other with their pincers to win a female for mating.

Fact file

Lived: St. Helena, South Atlantic Ocean

Habitat: Dry grassland, forest

Length: 3 in. (8 cm)

Diet: Leaves, flowers, fruit, fungi, insects

Extinct: 2014

The females looked after their young carefully. They cleaned their eggs and helped the baby earwigs to hatch out. They fed their young by coughing up food. The young stayed safe under their mothers' bodies.

When people first arrived on the island, mice and centipedes came with them. These predators ate the earwigs. The earwigs had no wings, so they could not escape by flying away.

People drove these insects to extinction. They took the stones covering the earwigs' burrows and used them for building materials.They cleared the forests where the earwigs lived.

Passenger pigeon

Ectopistes migratorius

- This sleek pigeon was built for speed. It had long, pointed wings and large chest muscles to power its flight over long distances. It could fly as fast as a car, at around 60 mph (100 kph).

- Passenger pigeons lived in vast flocks that could contain hundreds of thousands of birds. The flocks were so big that they sometimes took three days to pass overhead and blocked out the sun.

- At night, so many pigeons could crowd together on one tree that their weight broke the branches. Their shrieking, chattering, and clucking could be heard far away.

- Male and female passenger pigeons looked different. The males had pinkish-red breasts, which helped them to show off to females. They were also slightly bigger than the females.

- Flocks of passenger pigeons moved around with the seasons to find the best places for feeding and nesting.

- Around 500 years ago, passenger pigeons were the most common bird in North America. There were perhaps as many as 3 to 5 billion individual pigeons.

- In less than a hundred years, the numbers of pigeons crashed from billions to zero. The forests where they lived had been destroyed. People had also killed them for food or because they ate farm crops.

Fact file

Lived: Canada, USA, Mexico, Cuba

Habitat: Deciduous forest

Length: 16½ in. (42 cm)

Diet: Tree nuts, seeds, berries, worms, insects

Extinct: 1914

Falklands wolf

Dusicyon australis

🐺 The Falklands wolf was the only land mammal ever to live on the windswept Falkland Islands. It was a top predator that hunted alone.

🐺 This wolf's ancestors probably walked to the islands from mainland South America. During the last Ice Age 16,000 years ago, the shallow sea between the mainland and the islands froze over. This created an ice bridge for the wolves to cross.

🐺 Falklands wolves lived in burrows dug by penguins or other animals. They did not dig the burrows themselves.

This hunter came out to look for prey during the day. When it was looking for food along the coast, it often went swimming in the sea.

The Falklands wolf looked and behaved more like a jackal than a wolf. It had long legs like a jackal and did not hunt in a pack like a wolf.

The scientific name of the Falklands wolf means "foolish dog of the south."

People hunted the wolf for its valuable fur and to protect the sheep that they brought to the islands in about 1850. The wolf was not afraid of people, so it was easy to catch. By the mid-1870s, there were no Falklands wolves left.

Fact file

Lived: Falkland Islands (Malvinas)

Habitat: Rocky scrub, grassland, marshland, beaches

Length: 38 in. (97 cm)

Diet: Birds, seal pups, insects, fish, crabs, reptiles

Extinct: 1876

Carolina parakeet

Conuropsis carolinensis

🦜 The forests of the eastern United States once rang with the cries of these colorful parakeets. Huge, noisy flocks of up to 300 birds took to the air, screeching so loudly that they could be heard for miles.

🦜 During the heat of the day, the parakeets rested or sunbathed. In the morning and at sunset, they fed on the fruits and seeds of trees such as sycamore and cypress.

🦜 An adult Carolina parakeet weighed only as much as a hamster.

🦜 The Seminole people of southeast United States called the Carolina parakeet *puzzi la née*, which means "head of yellow."

🦜 The flesh of these parakeets was poisonous to predators. The poison came from the cocklebur seeds that the birds could eat without being harmed.

🦜 People loved to use the birds' colorful feathers to decorate hats. But to get the feathers, they killed the parakeets.

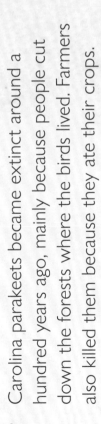 Carolina parakeets became extinct around a hundred years ago, mainly because people cut down the forests where the birds lived. Farmers also killed them because they ate their crops.

Fact file

Lived: Eastern USA

Habitat: Forests and swamps

Length: 12 in. (30 cm)

Diet: Seeds, fruits, flowers, buds

Extinct: 1918

Round Island burrowing boa

Bolyeria multocarinata

🐍 This snake squeezed its prey to death in its powerful coils. Then it opened its jaws very wide and edged the victim down into its mouth so it could swallow the body whole.

🐍 The Round Island burrowing boa was not a poisonous snake, so it did not have fangs. All of its teeth were the same size and curved backward to help the boa keep a firm hold of its prey. If any teeth were broken, new teeth grew underneath the old ones to replace them.

🐍 The boa's long, pointed snout helped it to burrow through the top layers of the soil on the tiny volcanic island where it lived.

Fact file

Lived: Round Island off Mauritius, Indian Ocean

Habitat: Forests, grassland with palm trees

Length: 3 ft. (1 m)

Diet: Lizards

Extinct: 1975

This snake began to die out about 180 years ago, after people brought goats and rabbits to Round Island. These animals ate the plants whose roots held the soil together. Most of the soil where the boa lived was washed away in the rain.

Although the Round Island burrowing boa was harmless to humans, people hunted this snake, which helped to drive it toward extinction.

Chiriqui harlequin frog

Atelopus chiriquiensis

Male harlequin frogs were mainly yellow or lime green. The larger females had colorful, boldly patterned skin, which gave these frogs their name. Harlequins were pantomine figures who wore diamond-patterned costumes.

These tiny frogs were only the size of an adult's thumb.

Glands on this frog's head and back produced powerful poisons. These helped to protect the frog from predators.

Fact file

Lived: Costa Rica

Habitat: Mountain rainforest, forest streams

Length: 1–2 in. (25–50 mm)

Diet: Insects

Extinct: 2020

The Chiriqui harlequin frog had webbed feet, which helped it to swim in forest steams. The feet were good at pushing the water aside, like the flippers worn by human swimmers.

In the breeding season, male Chiriqui harlequin frogs lived in their own area, or territory, next to a forest stream. They tried to keep rival males out of their territory with warning calls, but sometimes they had to fight.

The female Chiriqui harlequin frog laid hundreds of eggs at a time. The eggs were joined together in long strings. Each egg was protected by a jelly coating.

Chiriqui harlequin frogs became extinct mainly because of a deadly fungus disease, which stopped them breathing through their skin. Climate change probably helped the fungus to spread.

Western black rhino

Diceros bicornis longipes

 The western black rhino was really gray, but it loved to wallow in dark mud, which sometimes made its skin look black. The mud acted as a natural bug repellent and sunblock.

 This big, bulky animal could charge through the bush faster than any human sprinter if it was scared or angry. It ran on its toes and could suddenly change direction very quickly.

 The two pointed horns of this shy and secretive creature were made from hairlike strands of keratin pressed tightly together. Keratin is the same material your fingernails and hair are made of.

 Western black rhino calves were born without horns so that they would not injure their mother during birth. When the calves were one or two months old, their horns started to grow. They kept growing throughout the rhino's life.

Fact file

Lived: West Africa

Habitat: Grassland, woodlands, wetlands

Length: 10–12 ft. (3–3.5 m)

Diet: Leaves, branches, fruit

Extinct: 2011

Even though they had bad eyesight, western black rhinos could hear and smell very well. Their cone-shaped ears picked up even the faintest sounds.

People hunted the western black rhino to extinction for its horns. They used the horns in medicines, and made them into expensive handles for knives.